How to earn $100,000 Per Year

A Passive income guide for wealth and freedom

Copyright © 2019

All right reserved. No portion of this book may be reproduced, stored in a retrieval system, or transmitted in any form or by any means – electronic, mechanical, recording or otherwise – except for brief quotation in printed reviews without the prior written permission of the publisher or the author.

Table of Contents

INTRODUCTION 4
PART ONE: ONLINE OPPORTUNITIES 7
    GOOGLE ADSENSE 8
    AFFILIATE MARKETING 12
    BUILD AN ONLINE STORE OR BUY ONE 16
    CREATE A MOBILE APP 19
    PUBLISHING BOOKS 22
    SPONSORED POSTS 25
    WEBINARS 28
    PODCASTING 32
    YOUTUBE 35
    AN ONLINE COMMUNITY 38
PART TWO: OFFLINE OPPORTUNITIES 42
    REAL ESTATE 44
    THE STOCK MARKET NEVER GETS OLD 48
    INVEST IN A BUSINESS 51
    ANNUITIES 54
    PEER TO PEER LENDING 57
CONCLUSION 59

Introduction

Wealth creation is an aspiration everyone desires, we all want to earn more and do better with our finances, and the big question is "How?" In previous times, it was okay for a person to get a job and work hard while getting paid from one source of income, today the situation is different, and it is for the best.

People started to gain insight into the concept of passive income and how possible it is for a person to earn money without working actively or going to sit in an office. As passive income gained traction all over the world, a lot of individuals started to practice this form of wealth creation, and their success stories inspired others to take the plunge.

Who says you must sit still for hours working tirelessly till you make money? You can have it all; work and even get to make money passively on the side. Passive income helps you enjoy the job you love while creating wealth for multiple streams.

The objective of this book is to help you discover some of the most effective means of creating wealth through passive income. Now there are thousands of options for passive income all over the world, while we won't be able to provide insight into all of them, you will get to read through the most profitable and viable options available.

For a more robust experience with varying options, this book is divided into two parts; the first part focuses on passive income opportunities available online. The second part of the book is all about the avenues for businesses that can generate passive income offline.

The goal is to utilize a passive income opportunity that helps you earn up to $100,000 per year, and this goal is attainable if you are focused, determined and apply the right principles at the right time.

You can utilize both the online and offline opportunities at the same time, this is one of the most striking features about passive income; the ability to do so many things and earn from numerous income streams.

Alright, we are done with the introductory section; it is time to get started! Are you ready to grow your income streams now and become rich? I hear your loud "Yes!" let's get started with the first part of our journey that takes us into the world of online possibilities.

Part One: Online Opportunities

This first section takes you into the world of the internet as we dive into the openings available *online*. Technology has made it possible for individuals to render services and sell products across borders.

With several online payment options such as PayPal, there are minimal or no challenges with processing payments. Now regardless of what you do; a stay home mum, a businessman/woman, student or even a civil servant. You can earn up to $100,000 yearly implementing any of these online business ideas.

We must set the ball rolling now as we launch this first section with one of the most popular online go-to business ideas. Flip over to the next page to learn more about this leading passive income idea and how you can utilize it in creating wealth.

Google AdSense

If you have ever visited any website for information, shopping or just surfing the internet, you must have seen "Google ads." These ads are all up in your face, and they are making a lot of money from them passively.

The ads are straightforward to set up on any website, but for them to be on your site, you must have a steady amount of traffic. Google ads are opportunities for businesses to market their products and services to the broader world because everyone is online!

Google AdSense is very easy to set up; what you need is a website or a blog where you can sign up for a free Google AdSense Account. After signing up, Google will provide a code which you paste on your website, and then Google takes over the process from there by tracking your page views, earnings and views.

You don't have to pay for maintenance or pay anyone to keep things going for you on your website. The most fundamental part of the entire process is to get a website first and then work had to build it up to the point where you have a huge following and a consistent number of visitors daily.

Google AdSense helps you earn money without having to work for it, and this is to say that you don't work for the companies who advertise. You may, not be a fan of whatever they announce yet you get access to funds when their services, products, and offers are on your website.

Lots of bloggers attest to the fact that nothing beats the feeling of getting money from Google while going about their day. So, you need to focus on growing traffic to your website; concentrate on the content you should place on the site. The money will come to you after all the hard work you put in.

With Google AdSense, you will become a part of a network of people who contribute to connecting businesses to potential customers and getting paid for it. Depending on the number of visits you get on the site, it is possible for you to make more than $100,000 yearly from Google AdSense.

Create a website today if you don't have any if you have one already and you aren't gaining traffic, work on getting more traffic to your site and if you are already getting traffic to intensify your efforts to get more. Google AdSense is one of the most authentic ways of making cool passive income online.

Aside ads, there is another form of marketing that helps you earn money passively. You might want to guess what we will be discussing next, but what's the point in speculating when you can flip over to the next page and discover what we will be considering next.

Affiliate marketing

Affiliate marketing is also another online idea you should consider because you will be earning money just by linking users and consumers companies that provide what they need. With this passive income opportunity, you partner with brands and businesses whose products or services align with what the content on your website.

What you need to do is mention a product on your blog or website, provide a link to the product using the affiliate code you were given when you signed up and make money every time someone makes a purchase using your unique system.

Now the secret to being successful with affiliate marketing is to partner with brands whose products are strictly related to what you consistently post on your blog or website. If you always write about weight loss, then the companies you partner with for affiliate marketing should offer products that will help your readers or followers lose weight.

Aside from signing up for an individual affiliate account, you can benefit more from the affiliate ad network that provides lots of varying affiliates in one place. So, through the web, you get to see the products that work and the ones that do not work.

Prominent bloggers and web owners who optimize their content to suit the affiliate program earn more than $100,000 monthly. You can make money with any product that has a huge market base and is attractive to users. However, you must build a followership base as well just as it is with Google AdSense.

Every time someone clicks on the code on your blog and buys, BOOM, you get paid. This means that if 300 people use the code in one day, well I will allow you to do the Math.

What makes affiliate marketing work is a combination of:

1. A well-developed website/blog
2. Steady traffic
3. A great product (something your target audience cannot do without)
4. Insightful content that captivates your readers
5. Consistent effort.

Most times some other affiliates reach out when they see that you are making progress with the affiliates you work with. The more people you sign on, the more money and the more influence you garner. Affiliate marketing is gradually becoming the first option individuals consider when thinking about passive income online.

Did you know that you can make money just by creating an online store? The next idea will help you find your path to real wealth and lasting freedom.

Build an Online store or buy one

eCommerce is the way to go now; everyone can purchase items online at anytime from anywhere across international borders. So that means the online store owners are cashing out, are you thinking about Amazon right now? You should and then make up your mind to make the most out of your desire for passive income by building an online store or buying an existing one with customers.

With an online store, you don't have to buy products to sell, all you must do is create the right environment for sellers to come to present their products and services and then make money from the space they occupy in your store online.

Transactions are solely between the customers and the sellers, all you must do is ensure that the store is operational and that your users of the store do not complain about its interface. The more sellers use your store, the popular it becomes thus making it a desirable platform for other business owners.

You can work from anywhere, but if you want it to be solely a passive income option, then you can hand the business over to someone to manage while you continue to get cash for completed transactions.

Sometimes the fear of starting all over can be terrifying so instead of doing that you can buy an already existing business and remodel it the way you want to continue to build it up.

One thing is satisfied with a thriving online store, and you will always have consistent streams of income without having to sell anything or own a product line actively.

Make sure you operate a store that provides the essential items people cannot live without, this will make it a multi-purpose online store that is a one-stop fun shop for everything any anything!

While operating your online store, you can also do several other things that guarantee passive income and set up a mobile app is one of such ideas. The next part of this section will take you through the rudiments of setting up a mobile app and how you can earn passive income with the concept.

Create a mobile app

People are looking for solutions everywhere, but more importantly, they are looking for platforms that will make things easier for them. So, technology provides options, but within the pool of possibilities, there is the idea behind mobile apps which is one way to earn passive income.

This concept for this kind of passive income is that it is meant for those who are techies and people who love to experiment with technology. You will need the technical background to know the kind of app you want to build and how you want the user interface to be presented.

However, you should understand that before discussions on user interface and the type of app to create, you must carry out research that helps you determine what people need in a mobile app. The feedback you get from the public should be used to build an app that solves a problem.

You can either build an entirely new app or improve on an existing one; if you have a novel concept, you can experiment with it but if you feel like your idea is already in use, but you can make it better, do that.

Every app on your device is making money for someone somewhere. App investors can make as much as $1million after the successful launch of an app that is brilliantly presented.

Your passive income starts to trickle in as people download your app and this is how you build lasting wealth. Lots of people are making thousands of dollars monthly from apps they created so even if you don't start with millions; you can rest easy knowing that the money will build up gradually.

How much do you think founders of Instagram, Facebook or Twitter make monthly? Millions of people use these apps for personal and business opportunities, and this explains why you must get on with the app idea immediately.

If your app gets a lot of downloads from individuals, then you will also be able to cash in with ads that are paid for. Create an app that makes life easier for people, and you will always have enough cash to take care of your needs.

Remember that this idea is for those who are technology-inclined because there are lots of technical concepts to grasp. Can you write? If you answered in the affirmative, then the next idea is mostly suited for you as writing is an excellent source of passive income.

Publishing Books

Writing is such a useful skill that will help you cash in with passive income especially when you are talented in creating online content that gets the attention of readers. Freelance writing is a means to earn money and guess what? You can do it in your spare time.

With freelance writing, passive income becomes possible when you start creating content for clients who pay you for approved jobs and referrals help you retain clients. Now with the freelancer, you can start with websites such as www.upwork.com where you can secure writing gigs.

However, you need to find a niche for yourself, what are good at writing? What do you enjoy writing? What areas or genres capture your attention? If you don't figure out your niche, you will struggle.

You can earn as much as $20,000 monthly by creating original content for publications, magazines, authors, and individuals who want to have a book but can't write. Most freelance writers say the fact that they get to work from home at their convenience is one of the perks of the job.

More importantly, you can create different channels for your writing to take off speedily, so you enjoy multiple streams of income all at once. Now the idea for a passive income pattern is to do something that guarantees steady payment, and this is what writing will do for you.

You can also write a book and earn royalties from the publication, with this idea you need to discover what people want to read about the most. Carry out your research, write about it, publish the material and earn money on a steady basis.

With your book on platforms such as Amazon Kindle, you can be sure of steady income flow even years after publishing it. You see, writing opens doors for passive income, and these doors don't ever get closed because knowledge is forever.

If you cannot sustain the effort that comes with freelance writing long-term, you should write a couple of books, market and distribute them online. If your book deals with the issues people are concerned with daily, you can be sure that it will make sales and you will earn royalties for a long time. Now that is what passive income is about!

Another way to earn passive income online is through sponsored posts; if you have a social media following, then you are ready to make more money so head over to the next section now.

Sponsored Posts

Sponsored posts are quite like Google AdSense, but there is a difference, you will be handling the sponsors directly and negotiating your terms of payment and postings. Now as the name implies sponsored posts simple means someone pays you to place their content on your platform.

By "platform" we mean your blog, website or social media space. You can make a lot of money with just one post, and this sets the precedence for others to come your way. Companies are ready to pay bloggers to write something positive about their products and services which will translate into sales and public acceptance.

Since we are in the social media era, influencers on Twitter and Instagram also get paid to post about products. You can cash in just by having a large following on social media because companies want their products to be seen, heard and liked.

You have the number of people they need, so they sponsor your posts by paying you, and you do the needful on your page. Some influencers tend to charge around $4,000 for one post, if you go to an influencer's page and you spot the #ad on their job, then that is sponsored post.

You can promote companies you trust and build long-term relationships with organizations you can partner with all the time. Some bloggers also get $20,000 for sponsored posts and the higher your followers, the more money you can get.

With the sponsored post, you don't have to rely on a website because it is always more of social media where people can interact about the products and the company gets instant feedback. What you must do is build your social media following till you become an influencer who gets paid to sponsor posts.

You will not only get paid for posts, but you will also get a lot of free items, the things you promote will be given to you for free which makes it possible for you to test them before posting and encouraging followers to make a purchase.

If you have ever watched a webinar, you will agree that it is one of the most exciting ways to learn. Well, you can make passive income through webinars; all you must do is flip over to the next page to learn about this exciting opportunity.

Webinars

If you still in search for more ways to make money online, if you are looking for something you will be comfortable with, you might want to try webinars. Everyone loves free advice. I mean if you were to pay to watch something that will transform your life and get the same content for free you will probably go for the free offer, after all, it's the same.

With webinars, you can teach others, market your products, services, and an online course, it is akin to offering tips and strategies for free, but at the end, you can pitch your service with the aim to secure purchases and deals. With this online platform, you have to prepare something to offer and then hope that after your offering, the people who watch buy into the service you provide.

The process of creating a webinar can be daunting at first, so you might want to rely on online courses that teach how you can start on with a webinar. After working on your pitch, try to connect the subject matter of what you ate talking about to the product you want them to buy.

This is how you earn passive income from this, so some people might watch your webinar and not buy at first. But if the message or lesson was compelling enough, it will cause them to come back to make a purchase and even share the information with someone else who makes a purchase and just like that between one webinar and another one; you make money.

If you don't have a personal product or service to offer, you might refer to a sponsored product. Now this sponsored product is paid for by the sponsor who has partnered with you to advertise it. When people buy, you get a commission based on the number of people that buy from your webinar.

If you have been doing a lot of work already building your audience, you wouldn't have problems with this aspect of using webinars. Also, make sure that as you discuss on the webinar, you take your audience along with you by asking and answering questions.

When your subscribers ask questions that require you giving them advice, you can use the opportunity to introduce them to the product or service you are promoting. You don't have to wait until the end of the webinar to share ideas on the service or product; you can do it in between takes which is why Q&A sessions are so vital during webinars.

Podcasting is a brilliant way of bringing in passive income which is why we will be deliberating on how to podcast and make money in the next page.

Podcasting

Hosting a podcast is a sure way of earning passive income. Now if you have a blog, you can use it as an avenue to promote your podcast to your followers; by doing this, you will be getting more sponsors and advertisers to expand on your podcast.

Amelia a favorite podcaster got a sponsor who was willing to pay $5,000 to include a short clip at the start of her podcast for 60 days. Now think about this, at this time Amelia just started to try out the podcast idea, but because she had a considerable number of followers on her blog, the sponsors knew that the same people who create traffic to the blog would listen to her podcasts.

You can go ahead with your plans for your podcast by sharing whatever you think your ardent followers want to hear and by doing something as simple as that, money will find its way to your account passively.

If you want to succeed with podcasting, you must find your niche first, grow your audience and then seek ways to monetize by reaching out to sponsors. Although any podcaster will agree that it isn't the most natural way of making money online because you must record and edit but think about this option if you love podcasting, public speaking, and sharing.

Which is why podcasting is meant for those people who have a passion for it. If you do have a passion for podcasting, give it all you've got. Don't stop recording and sharing even if at first, it seems like no one is listening. The most fantastic thing you can experience online is to discover that all the effort you put in when it looked like no one was paying attention pays off eventually.

You will be amazed at the number of organizations and companies who will want just one minute of your podcast and pay handsomely for it. So sometimes you still get paid even when you haven't put out new material. Your money compounds with time, and before you know it, there is a list of sponsors just waiting for a "Yes" from you.

Something closer to podcasting also aids passive income a lot, and that is what we will discuss in the next part of this section.

YouTube

We all love YouTube. I mean where else can you get official videos if not YouTube? Well, you can make money passively from this platform through a YouTube Channel. With the channels, you get to talk about just about anything or share on any idea with your subscribers. As you share, you create an avenue through which money can be made.

The people on YouTube with the vast number of subscribers earn money in exchange for their videos and time. Some YouTube vloggers have built multi-millionaire business just by sharing with others in their spare time.

The more subscribers you have, the more likely it is for your channel to get ads which translate into a passive for you. The owners of the products or services to be promoted on your channel will pay because they are aware that if they can reach a percentage of your subscribers, they will be making a lot of sales.

This means that you must first have a YouTube channel where you share on whatever interests you or your subscribers and then work on building your subscriber base to have a lot of people. You can share a link to your channel on your social media pages, share with friends and continue to push for more people to watch you.

The long-term result of all the effort you put in is that you will attract ads even from Google. If you want to be like those YouTube stars who make a lot of money, you must take the first step and set up your channel.

After creating your channel, make sure you offer the most exciting video content that makes it easier for people always to come back to watch. Be aggressive with building your channel, and you will be able to sit still one day and enjoy the proceeds of being a vlogger.

Aside from YouTube, there are other options online available for anyone who wants to make passive income and one of such viable options is building an online community. The next part of this section will teach you more about this idea.

An online community

You can earn money online by creating an online community. Today, millions of people are online searching for different things; friendship, business, validation, romance, etc. Now you are also in search of something, so why not build an online community where people who are in the search like you find answers and bond?

Building online communities don't have to be restricted to creating blogs, we live in the age of social media, and there are more options for you to build an online space for people now. There is Twitter, Instagram, Facebook, and so many others. How can you make passive income through online communities?

Well, when you create a community with colossal followership or members, you also attract businesses who want to advertise. Always remember this on your pathway to being successful with passive income; anywhere you find many people, there is an opportunity to make money.

If you have a Facebook group for first-time mums or pregnant women, diaper companies and other organizations that produce items for nursing mothers and children will want to advertise with you.

You charge them per post and duration of the post, gradually you start to make money because the women who are in your group will make purchases and companies love purchases.

Promoting products never gets old when there are several platforms for promotion, it means people are cashing out already. If you have a personal social media and you don't want to use it for your online community, don't be afraid to create a new one and start all over again. If your group or community is engaging enough, it will attract your target audience.

You can promote your community, for example, you can improve your group's visibility on Facebook using Facebook Ad; this is an example of a measure you put in place to expand the reach of your community. The more visible your group is, the easier it is to get products you can promote.

So in your office, using your mobile phone, you can continue to connect community members while counting the monies that come in from product features. This is a consistent way of getting passive income in thousands of dollars. Ensure that you aren't restricted to just one social media platform or one online sector.

Some of your target audience may be on Twitter more than Facebook or on Instagram so "If" you can manage all, have multiple communities which also makes it possible for you to reach more people and guess what that translates into? More $$$$.

Building online communities bring us to the end of the first section; passive income via online platforms. The online space is so exciting right now because of the abundance of the opportunities and platforms available for anyone who wants to make money.

Remember to stick to platforms and options that work perfectly for you and, sit back, relax and count monies you make effortlessly. The next section takes you into the offline world; are you ready to make money from multiple sources? Flip over and enjoy the read.

Part Two: Offline Opportunities

Welcome to the second part of the journey to earning more, creating wealth and living free! In this section, you are going to discover ideas that will be helpful in generating passive income *offline*.

The concepts you will find below can be done without being on the internet 24 hours of the day and guess what? They are as profitable as the ideas you read through in the first part. We will begin right away with the real estate market; buying and selling properties is the new way to go!

*Please note that most of these offline businesses might take a long time for profits to start trickling in but when they do, it is always worth the wait. You might also need to discuss with professionals for some of the concepts before going ahead.

Real Estate

Real estate investing is a favorite way to make passive income these days, and surprisingly you don't have to own brick to become an investor. The world of real estate investment is gradually becoming more dynamic, so there are lots of options available for you to explore.

Firstly, you must be sure that you've got the passion for real estate investment and that you have the financial means to buy the properties. Although real estate requires a lot of time and work, if you put in the effort, it will yield positive results.

1. The "Buy and Hold" strategy

The first option for real estate investment through passive income is the "Buy and hold" option. As the name implies, this strategy entails you buying the rental property, renting it out to tenants who get to pay via a mortgage. As a landlord, you will generate passive income through rents while the property appreciates.

The buy and hold pattern are a long term investment plan that guarantees excellent returns if you have the best properties that are the right fit for tenants.

2. The "Raw land" strategy

This plan entails the purchase of lands without edifices that are bought at a lower price and then sold for at a time when the prices for land drops so the profit margin for sales increases. The most exciting fact about the raw land method is that you can choose to sell the property whenever you want to or sell off portions of it, regardless of how you make sales, this is one way of making money passively.

3. Short term rentals/Airbnb

It is possible to purchase a property, rent it out or just a part of it (maybe a room). Now for this strategy, the property you chose, should be in an area where tourists or visitors come often. Do your property serves as a short-term accommodation platform for the visitors.

If you offer attractive features such as complimentary breakfast, free wi-fi and other amazing things people like, your ratings can soar leading to referrals which translates to increased profit margins.

4. Properties with market values

You can make as much as $200,000 per a single transaction when you target properties with high market values. A lot of times, people who get involved with real estate do so by purchasing just about any property wonder why they don't make high sales.

Well, the solution to making amazing and sustainable sales is for you to set your eyes on properties with important market values. Such properties have peculiar features that make them appealing to buyers so with just one sale; you can achieve a lot of passive income.

Several opportunities in the real estate sector offer you outlets for passive income. Remember that you must have the passion for the industry and be committed to the process long-term. Regardless of how long it takes for a property to be sold when you do make a sale, it's going to be an impressive one.

The real estate market isn't the only area where you can enjoy passive income; flip over to the next page and gain access to a viable market that is hugely profitable.

The stock market never gets old

Another way to start earning money through passive income is by investing in the stock market which never gets old by the way. The stock market offers you the opportunity to spend money in companies you believe have a steady future and make money when the company hits enormous numbers.

With the stock market, your role is quite simple, search for stocks that are viable enough to invest with. You can rely on the advice of a stockbroker if you are not sure about the companies. Once you get a good organization to make an investment with, start small.

You can make a much more massive investment later when you reap the dividends of your investment. Earning $100,000 per annum with stocks wouldn't be a problem if you invest in industries that are profitable. Gradually, you will start to see your shares rise at some point and fall depending on the vulnerability of the market.

However, you can make passive income with stocks when you buy shares at their lowest prices, hold them for a while till they gain market value and then sell off when they increase in value. The only job you will be required to do is to monitor your stocks to be sure that you will be selling at the right time.

Stocks have been a significant source of passive income for a lot of people; you have the freedom to do whatever job you chose while accumulating wealth via shares from a company. With multiple shares, you increase your chances of earning more and gaining first-hand experience of how the stock market works.

There is a caveat though; the stock market is quite volatile, this means that it can all come crashing down before your very eyes. My advice is that you study the market for a while before you start trading and sell when it is an excellent time to do that.

Aside from its volatile nature, the stock market is an excellent choice for passive income any day. Can business investment be a good source of passive income? You've got to read the next point to discover answers.

Invest in a business

Another way to sustainable passive income is by investing in a company. There are millions of people who have ground-breaking ideas that will solve the problems of the world. But most of such idea's creators are unable to bring their business contents to life because of a lack of funding.

Now when some people hear about investing in a business, they automatically feel like they need to put in a lot of money to make it work and this is untrue. Some ideas require millions of dollars; some other ideas need a few thousand while some great ideas as well as can flourish with whatever you have set aside you invest.

Remember that with this idea, you might not be the only investor who invests in the start-up, but you can earn passive income when the business starts to flourish.

Before you throw in your investment funds, first determine how much you want to invest, then profile some start-up ideas you're considering looking out for their unique value proposition, target market, and profit-making plans.

If you are investing a lot of money, then you might want to discuss with a start-up expert that will provide professional insight into all aspects of the proposed business. If the business ticks all the right boxes, you can go ahead with your investment.

Now it might take a while for your investment to yield results because the business must break even first, gain a customer base and all other considerations. Eventually, you will get your initial investment and then regular additions as well.

Some businesses grow to become huge conglomerates and the bigger the company, the more money investors make. Pitch your tent with a viable idea that has a lot potential; you will be amazed at the level of progress you make with your investment.

Annuities

If you want to retire with a lot of money to fall back on then, you should consider annuities especially if you have been consistent with putting money into your 401(k). It is time to start thinking about your 60's when you want to quit working and live on passive income.

An annuity is a form of insurance or investment that makes an investor entitled to a series of monies annually. At the accumulation stage of annuity, you invest money like you would with a mutual fund and at a specific date, the contract "Annuities" thus making it possible for the investor to get regular payments.

Some investors use their annuity for retirement; they save and invest while they work and structure the annuity to pay them back after they turn 60 years of age.

Annuity returns can be used as a replacement for a paycheck, and there are of two types;

1. Variable Annuities

This type of annuity is structured; payments are made based on how the investments performed. This means that you will reap higher rewards when investments perform well and risk losing your money if the market doesn't play well.

2. Fixed Annuities

This annuity is a traditional type, instead of getting a specific investment, the institution pays fixed amounts periodically. Since most investors use this form as a retirement option, the monies can be spent when the investor wants it (preferably at retirement time).

Although annuities can be very expensive because of the numerous fees, you get to pay and commissions, yet it helps you save and invest in an account that is used continuously to invest thus helping you build income for years.

If you love accumulating interests over a long period, you will find the next passive income idea very appealing.

Peer to Peer Lending

Recently, investors are placing their monies in peer-to-peer lending companies; you will be lending your cash to peers via means of personal loans through which you earn interest. This process is like how banks and other lending organizations work, but there are designated sites you can site for lending to take place.

Sites such as www.lending.com and www.prosper.com/invest offer peer-to-peer lending services where accounts can be opened for investments to take place. With every investment, the returns you get varies but with the sites listed here you get a 5-10% return on the loans you give.

You also get to have a personal account where people looking for loans can connect with you. With Lending Club, your account will be in the "Prime" services they offer. So passive income is enjoyed when you borrow, get your money back with some extra percentage as interest.

Peer-to-Peer lending is becoming one of the most preferred options for passive income. Nothing beats the feeling of using your money to get more money without having to put in extra work.

With Peer-to-Peer lending, we have come to the end of the offline chapter but certainly not the end of this book. There is one more section you must read through, why? Because it contains an extraordinary message, you cannot afford to miss. Head over to the concluding part now!

Conclusion

The pathway to true lasting wealth no longer lies within having just one job; it is a process that entails utilizing multiple opportunities for growth and capacity building.

What we have achieved with this book is help you understand the possibilities that lie within doing what you love (which might be your present job) and having several other options that guarantee the creation of wealth.

The internet is replete with information quite like the content in this book, and millions of people use the internet so why are they not rich? You might wonder why there are fewer success stories about passive income, but the answer isn't so far-fetched.

There is a difference between knowing something and using it; some people say "Knowledge is power" but come on, it is the "Execution" of knowledge that is power. It isn't enough for you to know what to do until you take a step forward.

Now that you are armed with the right ideas and information, the billion-dollar question is this; what are you going to do? Wealth is a product of views, but those ideas must come alive in motion through execution. If you are not doing anything about what you know, you will be doing yourself a great disservice.

You have with you, a material that has the potential to transform your life forever, don't sleep on this information. Scan through the different options again and decide on what you think will work best for you.

After making your decision, go right ahead and start making plans.

You will encounter some setbacks at the beginning; you might feel overwhelmed wondering if you should continue with the path but don't give in to the problems. Great businesses are built with on the foundation of two words; PATIENCE AND DETERMINATION.

Have a goal in mind, something you want to achieve with your passive incomes. Your goal might be to buy a new home, travel to exotic places, get another degree, set up a much store, etc. whatever you want to attain with the monies accrued from passive income should always be in focus for you.

With a goal in mind, you will be inspired to hold on and not give up when it seems like it is becoming even more challenging to maintain the process. More importantly, you should remember that sustainability is vital for wealth creation.

All you have learned and all you have been exposed to through the sections above prepares you for a greater future with limitless options for wealth. Whatever field of business you decide to focus on, don't get started immediately; carry out in-depth research, get the right registrations and legal documents (if required) in place and blaze the trail of success and wealth through passive income.

I cannot wait to read your testimonials of success through passive income; it will be a source of inspiration to others who aspire to earn more. Thank you for being such a good sport by staying true to this journey till now, it gets better from this point.

Best wishes.

www.ingramcontent.com/pod-product-compliance
Lightning Source LLC
Chambersburg PA
CBHW040236220526
45473CB00001B/269